Science & Faith

Road to Harmony

by

Robert L. Piccioni, Ph.D.

D1738046

Science & Faith
Road to Harmony

Real Science Publishing
3949 Freshwind Circle
Westlake Village, CA 91361, USA

Edited by Joan Piccioni

Visit our web site:

www.guidetothecosmos.com

PREFACE

I believe science and faith are compatible.

While some seem to enjoy creating division and conflict — call them "Dividers" — they constitute a small minority. I believe most of us are people of good will, who prefer the harmony of mutual respect and identifying common ground.

No one need choose *either* science *or* faith and be compelled to reject the other. Rather, we can wisely combine science and faith to benefit everyone.

Most of this book discusses science, since that is my expertise. For those unfamiliar with science and its methods, I explore what science is, what it isn't, and its strengths and weaknesses.

Ideally, I would spend equal time discussing faith. But I am not a theologian, and there are too many different faiths to allow an equitable treatment of each. Instead, I rely on quotations from a few prominent religious leaders.

In seeking common ground between science and faith, I advocate for science, but not against faith. My sincere intention is not to contest the religious beliefs of others, nor to promote my own.

At this book's end, there are several appendices exploring key scientific theories and their supporting evidence. These appendices are for those who seek a better understanding of what science believes and why.

Table of Contents - 1

Chapter   Page

Table of Contents - 2

Table of Contents - 3

Appendices & More   Page

Chapter 1

Truth Cannot Contradict Truth

"All religions, arts and sciences
are branches of the same tree."
— Albert Einstein

Science and Faith *are* compatible. Both are sincere efforts to seek Truth, something we all value.

In 1996, Pope John Paul II convened an international conference of secular scientists. His opening address was titled: "Truth Cannot Contradict Truth."

He explained that whenever the truth of nature (as determined by scientists) seems to contradict the truth of scripture (as determined by clergy), our human understanding of one, or the other, or both must be in error.

His reasoning was that since God created both nature and scripture, the two cannot conflict.

Implicit in this view is that no one, neither scientist nor clergy, has the power to *dictate* truth. Truth is immutable. We can only hope to *discover* truth.

Sincere people of good will should not strive to win debates or vanquish opponents, but rather to understand the truth of our existence. This common goal *should* unite us. Yet, too frequently we seem antagonistically divided.

The divisiveness of our society pains me. I cringe when major issues are decided by a Senate vote of 51 to 49, or a Supreme Court vote of 5 to 4. I admit it hurts a bit less if "my side" wins.

From a broader view, the 5-to-4's average out over time with the 4-to-5's, but the animosities increase either way. Government is replete with Good Republicans and Good Democrats who unquestioningly vote their party line. Dividers inflame passions for their own purposes and squeeze out non-zealots.

Most Americans, I believe, have centrist views. What we most desire is a tranquil, stable environment in which we can raise our families. We need more Good Americans in office who will vote for everyone's best interests. I have no hope of fixing that.

There is, however, another regrettable social division that is entirely unnecessary that I think can be healed: the conflict between science and faith. I plan to sit astride the dividing wall, gradually chipping away, hoping to make some small difference.

Why does this wall exist? In part due to some misconceptions, and in part due to a few Dividers on each side whose personal interests are served by dispute.

Sadly, in our society, shock, confrontation, and sensationalism are money-makers. This is confirmed by the contents of newspaper headlines, TV sound-bites, radio talk shows, and popular movies. Provocateurs who denounce God or denounce science garner profit and celebrity. These Dividers prove only that every large group has its share of polemics.

Certainly it's easy to identify differences between

science and faith, but that occurs in all human affairs. The only person who never disagreed with me was my two-week old grandson Hunter ... and that didn't last.

We cannot require complete agreement as a precondition for cooperation.

Instead of obsessing over differences, let's focus on common ground. Our society has real issues to resolve. Americans, and indeed all civilized peoples, have real enemies and real challenges. We need as many friends as possible.

William Stoeger, a Ph.D. physicist and Jesuit priest at the Vatican Observatory, gave an intriguing lecture that I attended. He said something profound that I couldn't write down fast enough. The gist was:

Science and faith are each *never-ending* quests for the *least inadequate* description of Truth.

I wasn't surprised at his description of science. Science will always have unanswered questions, and scientists hope we are inching ever closer to nature's ultimate truth. But, I was surprised and pleased that he said the same about faith.

If we agree that no one has all the answers, and that we all sincerely seek truth, then why can't we get along?

I think most people believe science and faith can be compatible, despite the Dividers. Most people in developed countries accept major scientific discoveries — few still believe that a flat Earth is the center of the universe. And, many scientists are people of faith.

The two greatest scientists in history, Sir Isaac Newton and Albert Einstein, both believed in God (perhaps nontraditionally). And, according to a poll by Pew Research reported in the Los Angeles Times, 51% of scientists said they believe in a divine power, when asked privately. (I doubt that many would stand up and say so at a scientific conference. It is sad that they feel the need to hide their beliefs.)

In the remainder of this book, I hope to show that science is not an assault on faith. Science strives for an understanding of nature, something no one can dictate, but from which we can all benefit. Science should not be feared any more than scalpels; we just need to use both wisely.

Chapter 2

What Science Is

This chapter examines what science is, what we can expect from science, when we can rely on science and when we can't, and its strengths and weaknesses.

Science is society's organized effort to understand nature and to find ways to modify nature to our advantage. Science is driven by mankind's insatiable need to know: Why?

Most children ask *why* seemingly incessantly. They devote enormous effort trying to comprehend the rules of nature, how toys and products work, and the rules of our society.

Some children eventually stop asking why, perhaps because grown-ups tire of answering. Other kids never lose their innate curiosity and never stop wondering why; they become scientists.

LEARNING WITH OBSERVATIONS & MODELS

Science strives to understand nature by recording observations and by creating mental *models* (theories). Understanding comes when our models match our observations. Science cannot get far by observations alone, nor by models alone.

Only when models provide an insight that observations confirm does science take a great leap forward.

Before becoming generally accepted, observations must be repeated and confirmed by several independent groups. This eliminates inadvertent errors and the rare cases of fraud.

Scientists are not immune from the usual human failings. Occasionally, someone falsely claims spectacular results. This may be driven by excessive exuberance, or by venal motives, such as the pursuit of fame, promotion, funding, political correctness, or the validation of personal prejudices.

Fortunately, lying about nature never works. All observations are routinely repeated by other scientists in other countries with other agendas.

Science has a zero tolerance policy for deliberate falsification of data.

Thus, confirmed observations are highly reliable; these aren't opinions, these are facts of nature. Trying to deny a fact of nature is like trying to stop the rising Sun — one's energy is better spent elsewhere.

We know with great precision the age of the Earth (4.569 billion years) and the age of our universe (13.8 billion years). Those claiming everything was created 5778 years ago place themselves in an untenable position.

But, observations alone are not enough. It is interpretation that breathes life into observation.

What we really want to know is: what do the data mean?

For example, ten scientists might precisely measure the speed of light in various conditions. Those data alone are of limited interest. But, when Albert Einstein said the speed of light is the same in all conditions, the combination of observation and interpretation had profound impact.

As essential as interpretations are, they are less certain than are observations. Interpretations are based on models, mental constructs that we devise to "explain" what we see.

Constructing mental models of our environment is a hallmark of our species. Models allow us to predict what will likely occur in various situations, thereby helping us avoid hazards and achieve goals.

Superior models created by our greater intelligence enabled mankind's survival and lifted us to the top the food chain.

Yet, models are, after all, our best guesses, often very informed guesses, but guesses nonetheless. Models evolve due to increased insight or new and more precise observations.

VALIDATING EFFECTIVE MODELS

Over the last four centuries, a general approach to understanding nature has become widely accepted. This is not to say that no other way is possible; rather, our predecessors achieved more success when they followed the *scientific method* described below.

<u>Scientific Method</u>

1. Create a *model* to explain a specific natural phenomenon.

2. Find *unique predictions* of that model.

3. Test those predictions with *observations*.

4. *Validate* or *Falsify* the model.

5. *Report* results.

6. *Repeat.*

Scientists use the word "observation" in a broad sense that includes measurement, experimentation, or any similar gathering of data about nature.

Let's try an example.

Since the dawn of recorded history, people have wondered what material bodies are ultimately made of — if we cut something into ever-smaller pieces, will we ever come to an "end." Is water simply water, or is it ultimately made of tiny discrete parts that are somehow linked together?

Democritus, an ancient Greek philosopher and scientist, is credited with being the first to name these ultimate pieces of everything, calling them *atomos*, a Greek word meaning uncuttable.

For 2500 years, no one had the instruments or the genius to definitively prove that atoms do, or do not, exist.

Then in 1827, botanist Robert Brown used a microscope to observe tiny pollen grains suspended in water. Brown saw the pollen grains moving erratically with no discernible cause.

This phenomenon, later called Brownian Motion, remained a mystery for many generations.

In 1905, Einstein created a model to resolve Brownian Motion. In Einstein's model, pollen grains jumped when impacted by atoms, tiny particles too small to be seen.

Einstein derived precise predictions for the motions of these pollen grains in a variety of conditions. Others performed exacting experiments comparing Einstein's predictions to what actually happened in nature. The experiments confirmed Einstein's predictions, thus validating the model that atoms exist.

Step 6 merits discussion. If observations contradict a model's predictions, that model definitively does not explain nature and must be discarded. We must then go back to step 1 and find another model.

Conversely, if observations confirm a model's predictions, the model is validated in certain conditions to a certain level of precision. We must then repeat the process, testing more of the model's predictions in more circumstances to greater precision.

This process never ends. We can never assume a model is correct beyond the limits to which it has been validated by observation.

Note that a scientific model must make unique predictions that are *falsifiable* — it must be possible to prove the model wrong if it doesn't match nature.

Nobel Laureate Richard Feynman, my professor at Caltech, said: "The basis of science is its ability to predict."

A model that makes no testable predictions, or none that differentiate it from other models, is not useful science.

VALIDATION IS NOT PROOF

It is important to understand that scientists never prove anything in the same manner that mathematicians prove theorems.

The ancient Greeks proved the theorem that the sum of the interior angles of every triangle is 180 degrees. This theorem is still true 25 centuries later, and will be true forevermore. Theorems need to be proven only once.

However, this theorem assumes an ideal, Euclidean geometry. No one has ever proven that this theorem applies to the real world we live in.

It turns out, for most applications, the sum of the interior angles of any triangle is extremely close, but not exactly, 180 degrees. The theorem isn't wrong, but the geometry of the real world isn't perfectly Euclidean. We live on a spherical planet, in a universe of curved spacetime, where the geometry in most places is almost, but not exactly, Euclidean.

Mathematics can never prove a scientific model is true. Newton's laws of motion and gravity are mathematically perfect, but they do not properly describe nature.

Only experiments can tell us if it is a good model, and experiments are inevitably limited in precision and scope.

Imagine, for example, a factory that produces yardsticks. Let's test the model that all their yardsticks are "identical."

Experiments can easily determine if two yardsticks are the same length to one sixteenth of an inch. Using better instruments, we could measure them to one thousandth of an inch, or even to one millionth of an inch.

If the yardsticks happen to have significantly different lengths, we can hope to falsify the model that they are "identical". But if they differ infinitesimally, or not at all, we can never prove they are *exactly* the same length.

Experiments are also limited in scope: we can't measure yardsticks at absolute zero temperature or in absolute zero gravity.

As Einstein said: "No amount of experimentation can ever prove me right; a single experiment can prove me wrong."

Scientists can never say our theories are *proven*. Instead, we must say a model is *effective* in specified conditions, to a specified precision.

For example, Newton's Laws are effective through-out our Solar System, for all objects moving slower than one million miles per hour, to a precision of five digits (one part in 100,000).

For the vast majority of applications, Newton's Laws are entirely adequate. We use them to design perfectly satisfactory airplanes, bridges, buildings, and billiard tables.

But, where gravity is much stronger than our Sun's, or for objects moving at nearly light's speed, or when greater precision is needed, we must use Einstein's theories of relativity for their broader scope, higher precision, and more profound understanding.

While scientists can never claim our models are perfect, we have validated some to extraordinary degrees.

Quantum mechanics and special relativity have been tested tens of thousands of times, in every possible condition, and to extreme precision. None of the predictions of these theories has ever been proven wrong.

Quantum mechanics is validated to as many as 12 digits (one part per trillion). Special relativity is validated to as many as 18 digits (one part per million, trillion).

I claim nothing else we know about our real world is more thoroughly tested and more precisely confirmed that these two pillars of 20th century physics. These are as close to Truth as anything humans know about our physical existence.

Chapter 3

What Science Isn't

Science is neither authoritarian nor democratic.

Science has no leadership empowered to dictate scientific truth. We have no President with executive authority, no Pope, no Senate, and no Supreme Court.

Even Albert Einstein, the most esteemed scientist of all time, was demonstrably wrong about half the time. His mistakes didn't impede the advance of science because he had no more authority than any other scientist. Others corrected his errors and science moved forward.

Baseball fans' admiration of Babe Ruth isn't diminished by his 1330 strikeouts; neither is physicists' admiration of Einstein. But his mistakes prove that no single scientist, or group of scientists, can be relied upon to decide what is true.

Science does not accept expert opinion or testimony, written or oral. Even the most heart-felt sworn statement from the most esteemed scientist carries no weight of evidence.

Science also holds no democratic elections to determine scientific truth. On numerous occasions, the adamant convictions of nearly every scientist were later proven wrong.

How then is scientific truth established?

The only vote that counts is that cast by nature. Truth is what we observe actually occurring, and only what we observe.

No scientist can dictate what nature's truth is or what it should be; we can only hope to discover what it actually is.

The standard of proof in science far exceeds that of our legal system, political system, or indeed any other field of human endeavor. Only that which can be reproducibly observed by any competent person, anywhere, anytime, is acceptable scientific evidence.

Non-scientists might imagine that science is a tight-knit fraternity of good old boys closing ranks to oppose outsiders. Far from it. Scientists are more competitive than collegial. They compete for scarce jobs, tenured university professorships, limited funding, fame, glory, and the reluctant esteem of their peers.

Highlighting other scientist's mistakes is not discouraged; quite the contrary, proving others wrong enhances a scientist's career.

There is no faster path to success in science than disproving its most cherished pillars: special relativity and quantum mechanics. This may be one reason these theories have been tested so often.

Thus, no scientist, no group of scientists, and not even all the world's scientists acting in unison, have the power to dictate what is true. We can only observe nature, propose explanations, and report how well those explanations replicate nature.

SCIENCE IS NOT AN IMPEDIMENT TO FAITH

Science is also not a major reason for rejecting God, as is often claimed.

Every religious leader with whom I've spoken agrees that science is not a major impediment to faith. After all, the majority of scientists do believe in a divine power.

Rather, each of these religious leaders told me that the greatest obstacle to faith is the existence of evil and injustice.

Hasn't everyone at one time or another asked themselves: if God is benevolent, omniscient, and omnipotent, why do innocent children die? Why the bubonic plague? Why Auschwitz?

Some people can accept that evil can coexist with a benevolent God. Some can't.

Chapter 4

Strengths & Weaknesses of Science

Science has proven itself to be humanity's most effective means of understanding our physical world. It provides intellectual gratification, as do art, music, literature, and other endeavors. And, science is also the greatest engine of our physical and economic well-being.

ECONOMIC BENEFITS OF SCIENCE

Economists say science and technology have contributed 75% of the increased national wealth of the U.S. during the last 100 years, according to a study published in the Los Angeles Times in 2004. That study listed these telling facts about the U.S. in 1904:

1. Average life expectancy was 47 years.
2. Average annual income was $300.
3. 8% of homes had a telephone.
4. A cross-country one-minute phone call cost two days pay.
5. 14% of homes had a bathtub.
6. 144 miles of paved roads in all of U.S.
7. 6% of adults graduated from high school.
8. 10% of doctors had ever attended college.

The above could describe some of today's poorest and least developed countries.

I am amazed how much progress we have made in 100 years. Hopefully, today's poorest countries can also progress as rapidly.

The 25% of our improvement that economists didn't attribute to science and technology they attributed to capital investment. Buying a second mule increases farm productivity, but developing tractors is even more effective.

SCIENCE ANSWERS NUMERICAL QUESTIONS

As a broad generalization, science excels in addressing questions whose answers are numbers. We measure and compute superbly. Science is our best approach to determine:

1. The distance to the Sun
2. The age of the Earth
3. The age of mankind
4. The size and age of our universe

Here's an interesting example. In 1987, astronomers saw a new, amazingly bright star in the night sky. It was a supernova, the explosive death of a mammoth star. Supernovae can, for a brief time, emit as much light as 100 billion normal stars; they are among our universe's most violent events. Named SN1987a, this explosion was the nearest supernova since the invention of the telescope 400 years ago. Astronomers across the world rushed to study its every detail.

Dying stars typically cast off some of their outer layers before their climactic demise. Indeed, a ring of gas was seen around this star. That ring lit up like a Christmas tree 245 days after the initial supernova explosion.

The ring brightened when it was hit by the supernova's blast of light. This tells us that the ring was 245 light-days from the star (one light-day is the distance light travels in one day, which is about 16 billion miles). That distance combined with the difference in our viewing angle, from one side of the ring to the opposite side, determines our distance from SN1987a. That angle, labeled "a" in Figure 1, is about 8 micro-radians.

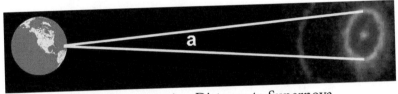

Figure 1: Measuring Distance to Supernova

By simple trigonometry, the distance D to SN1987a equals:

D = Ring Radius / tangent(a/2)

D = 245 Light-Days / 0.000,004

D = 168,000 Light-Years

One light-year is the distance light travels in one year, which is about 6 trillion miles. This means the measured distance from Earth to SN1987a is about 1 million, trillion miles.

The precision of this measurement is ±2%.

The prior analysis also means the light we saw from the supernova explosion took 168,000 years to reach Earth. Hence, the explosion that we saw in 1987 actually occurred 168,000 years earlier.

This is compelling evidence that the universe is at least 168,000 years old. In fact, we know from other measurements, which we will discuss later, that the universe is actually 13.8 ± 0.06 billion years old, a precision of about 0.4%.

DOES SCIENCE EXCLUDE GOD?

Some criticize science for excluding God from its considerations, equating this to rejecting God's existence. It is true that God does not explicitly appear in any scientific equation or theory. But, don't blame this on scientists; we report what we observe and what we don't.

If events beyond any naturalistic explanation did occur consistently and reproducibly, scientists would eagerly and meticulously analyze, document, and report these phenomena. If miracles of biblical proportion occurred today, scientists would rush to bear witness — what could be more exciting?

During the age of modern science, it seems God has not overtly intervened in any observable, reproducible manner that has yet been detected. (I am excluding paintings that shed tears, but are not available for scrutiny.) Absence of proof is not proof of absence, but consistent absence is a significant observation.

Restricting science to naturalism is essential in defining its scope. Science is a human endeavor, the pursuit of human understanding of nature and how mankind can modify nature for our benefit.

No person may define the role of God, but we should define our own roles.

For example, if doctors and scientists assume cancer is supernatural, beyond the realm of human understanding and control, cancer treatment and research would be futile — who got sick and who survived would be up to the supernatural, entirely out of our hands.

Instead, doctors and scientists assume cancer is within the scope of human endeavor, and that we can at least hope to eventually understand its causes and find cures.

The naturalistic approach to cancer is working. While still far from fully successful, we have made very significant progress; hundreds of thousands of people are alive today because of successful cancer research and treatment.

This is not to say that science has proven that God has no role in battling cancer. If God created the universe and all natural phenomena, cancer must be part of that creation, and human capabilities to mitigate cancer must also be part of that creation. With the incredible talent and determination that humans are born with, would not God be disappointed if we failed to do everything we could to aid those stricken by cancer?

Are we to believe that God created us to simply stand by and watch?

WHAT SCIENCE CANNOT DO

As great as science is with numbers, it is equally useless in other areas.

Every field of human endeavor has limitations: art is not very useful while performing open-heart surgery, and the world's best surgeons aren't typically our best artists.

Science is of very little value in answering questions such as:

1. Why was the universe created?
2. What is the purpose of our existence?
3. What is love?
4. Does God exist?
5. Which vision of God is closest to truth?

To most people, these questions are more important than knowing the precise age of the Earth. But science has no answers for such questions. For most people, the answers come through faith.

Another vital area that science can't address is morality. Science focuses on understanding nature, which has no moral compass. In nature, the fit survive and the weak perish, virtually without exception — it is eat, or be eaten. Concepts such as mercy, justice, and decency simply do not exist in nature.

How can people decide what principles they should live by? Moral codes can be established without reference to religious doctrine. But, for the vast majority of people, morality is defined by the teachings of their faith.

Judeo-Christian morality has been enshrined in the customs and laws of Western Civilization for more than a thousand years.

Morality based on religious teachings is the core of what we consider civilized behavior, the basis of most interpersonal interactions, and the essence of what we believe distinguishes us from less civilized beings.

Morality and ethics don't emerge from scientific equations; they originate with faith.

Chapter 5

Critique of "Science Disproves God"

Some claim modern science has proven that God does not exist, or that God is unnecessary.

The truth is that science has not proven, and will never be able to prove, that God does not exist. As to whether or not God is necessary, this is also a question science can never answer — it is an act of faith either way.

Proving scientifically that something does not exist is almost impossible. Scientists believe a single electrical charge can never be created nor destroyed. But, what we really know is that we have never observed a single charge being created or destroyed, and we know that cannot happen more often than one in a trillion times, or one in a trillion, trillion times, or even less. But we cannot say with certainty that it absolutely *never* happens.

Ancient peoples once believed that our Sun was a god who traveled daily across our sky. Science has shown that the Sun is really an immense ball of extremely hot gas, and that it is Earth that circles the Sun.

We understand the motions of celestial bodies with our theories of gravity. Does that prove there is no God, or does that prove that God created the laws of gravity?

The point is that no matter what science discovers, it will always be possible to say we discovered another part of God's creation.

God's existence is a matter of faith not science.

My book *"Can Life Be Merely An Accident?"* is a scientific analysis of the origin of the first life. I compute the probability that life could have originated spontaneously anywhere in our observable universe through any known chemical or physical process. That probability is ludicrously absurd, less likely than drawing the ace of spades 119,000 times in a row. If you prefer, the odds are 1 in a number N that has over 200,000 digits.

I don't claim to know how life did originate. Many attribute that to God. Their belief is an act of faith that science can neither prove nor disprove. Others believe science will one day discover a naturalistic, God-less mechanism for life's origin. Their belief is also an act of faith that science can neither prove nor disprove.

Some famous scientists have proposed a naturalistic answer to the extraordinary improbability of life originating spontaneously. They claim an infinite number of other universes exist beyond our own. And, they say, everything, including the extraordinarily improbable, must occur somewhere in an infinity of universes. They claim this proves God is unnecessary.

While an interesting conjecture, their work is opinion, not science. Not one shred of evidence exists to support the claim that other universes exist — they may well exist, but that is an unsubstantiated assumption.

In all likelihood, we will never know if other universes exist beyond our own observable universe — that's really the definition of "observable" — hence their assumption can never be substantiated.

Their claim that everything must occur in an infinite number of universes is also unprovable.

Infinity is sometimes used as an intellectual carpet under which some people sweep topics they'd rather not discuss. Invoking infinity is often a cop-out; it provides no useful information, and is merely a thoughtless way to avoid questions that deserve real answers.

Also, infinity is more complex than simply "everything that could possibly be." For example, the prime numbers are an infinite set of integers that contains only one even integer. Therefore, there are an infinite number of even integers not included in the infinite set of primes. So are an infinite set of multiples of 3, and of 5, and so forth. In fact, there are an infinite number of sets of integers, each infinitely large, that are not included in the infinite set of primes.

Even if there are an infinite number of other universes, ours might be the only universe that contains life. The claim that life must spontaneously arise somewhere in an infinite number of universes is an assumption that science can neither prove nor disprove. These assumptions are those authors' acts of faith, which are no more valid and no less valid than anyone else's act of faith.

I offer one final criticism of those who claim everything exists somewhere in an infinite number of universes. Even if one accepts all their unprovable assumptions, their final logic is flawed.

They claim their argument proves God is unnecessary. But, if every imaginable thing, regardless of how improbable, must exist somewhere, then God must also exist somewhere. What their assumptions demand is actually that God *is* necessary.

Others claim God does not exist because various miracles attributed to Him in Holy Books are scientifically impossible. While the latter may be true, we should consider the eras and objectives of Holy Books. Most preceded modern science by at least a thousand years. They were intended to teach morality to peoples who generally were uneducated, illiterate, and unprincipled. The Holy Books achieved their primary objective and greatly advanced civilization, even if some of their parables are fictional.

I have no quarrel with scientists, or anyone else, proclaiming their opinions — freedom of speech and freedom of religion are two of our most precious rights. But, opinions and beliefs should not be misrepresented as science or as more valid than the opinions and beliefs of non-scientists.

If scientists wish to enjoy public trust we must conform to professional standards of conduct. Professional athletes are not permitted to wager on their games. Judges must not decide cases involving personal interest. Conversely, politicians have lower standards, and as a result, aren't accorded the same public trust.

Scientists must choose where they wish to fit into that spectrum; they can't be impartial experts while campaigning for partisan beliefs.

Chapter 6

God of the Gaps

Henry Drummond was a 19th century evangelist. He cautioned people of faith not to tie their belief in God to what science cannot answer.

There will always be gaps in scientific knowledge, he said, but do not "fill these gaps with God" — do not believe these gaps prove God's existence.

As science advances, as it always does, it will eventually close some of these gaps. Those who took these gaps as proof of God will have their faith challenged.

Consider lightning as an example. Since mankind first existed, lightning has brought terrifying and inexplicable devastation. Many peoples tried to rationalize lightning as the wrath of God. Figure 2 shows Zeus armed with lightning bolts.

But the notion that lightning was God's wrath was troublesome, particularly since it often hit tall pointed buildings, such as churches.

Why would God destroy churches?

Eventually, science discovered that lightning is the discharge of static electricity and that tall, pointed steeples provide the optimum discharge path. We learned how to use lightning rods to protect ourselves, our houses of worship, and other buildings.

Those invested in lightning as a direct act of God were challenged by strong scientific evidence to the contrary. Alternatively, those believers who viewed God as creator of the universe, the laws of nature, and all we see, were unconcerned when science understood another of God's creations.

German theologian Dietrich Bonhöffer, from the depths of a Nazi prison, wrote:

"We are to find God in what we know,
not in what we do not know."

Figure 2: Zeus bearing lightning bolts

Chapter 7

Science & the Wonder of Existence

"There are only two ways to live your life.
One is as though *nothing* is a miracle. The
other is as though *everything* is a miracle."

— Albert Einstein

Some feel the wonder of God's creation is diminished by the "excessive" rationalism of science. Most scientists, I'm sure, believe the opposite — the more we learn, the more amazed we become.

WONDERFUL HUMAN BODY

Science has discovered much about the inner workings of the human body. Our bodies contain ten trillion human cells, and a much larger number of bacterial cells that mostly contribute to our mutual survival. Ten trillion is an enormous number, more than the number of stars in even the largest galaxy.

While stars do not work together for their galaxy's survival, every part of our bodies fulfills an essential function that is superbly coordinated throughout our entire lifetimes.

Our bodies replace millions of cells that die every second.

Our cells are fed and cleansed by 60,000 miles of blood vessels. Our hearts pump two quarts of blood every minute, and beat three billion times without fail. Command and control are accomplished with 45 miles of nerve fibers, connecting 100 billion neurons.

We all start as a single egg cell, about the width of a single hair, and self-assemble according to an internal blueprint.

Knowing how it works truly does make the human body all the more wondrous.

HEAVENLY STARS

Mankind has always been fascinated with stars, even elevating them to "heavenly" status. But what science has learned about stars is even more marvelous: all of us are stars — or at least, we are all made of stardust.

When the universe began, the only atoms that existed were hydrogen, helium, and just a dash of lithium — not adequate to form any kind of life whatsoever. There wasn't a single atom of carbon in the entire universe, and you'd have to hold your breathe for 300 million years to inhale the first oxygen atom.

The atoms of life are created in stars. As immense clouds of these primordial small atoms collapse, temperatures in the clouds' centers soar. Wherever the core temperature reaches 20 million degrees, nature's ultimate fire, nuclear fusion, ignites and a star is born. (Appendix F explores this further.)

Nuclear fusion is immensely more efficient than the fires we burn on Earth. It releases 15 million times more energy per pound than gasoline. Nuclear fusion is nature's way of making energy, of lighting the heavens, and providing life-sustaining warmth.

Through nuclear fusion in stars, small atoms merge together and create larger atoms: carbon, iron, oxygen, calcium, and all the other elements essential for life.

As their final gift, when stars run out of fuel and die, they cast off their outer layers and the most mammoth stars explode in cataclysmic supernovae. These most violent events in our universe disperse the precious atoms created inside stars, seeding other gas clouds that subsequently form new stars, new planets, and ultimately us.

Of all Earth's atoms, 99.99% (by mass) were created in stars. And 90% of the atoms in our bodies were also created in the centers of mammoth stars at temperatures of hundreds of millions of degrees.

We truly are made of stardust, the most rare and precious jewels that our universe struggled to produce for nearly 14 billion years.

The twinkle in your loved one's eye truly is a little bit of a star.

AMAZING EARTH

People have long recognized that our planet is a wonderful habitat, even if it is a step down from the Garden of Eden.

Scientific discoveries show Earth is even more amazingly wonderful than mankind initially thought.

First, we realized Earth is the best of our Solar System's 8 planets (9 if you're still counting Pluto). And even after astronomers found nearly 4000 exoplanets (those orbiting other stars), we still have not found any better habitat.

In other books, I explore in detail 14 remarkable characteristics of Earth and its environment that enable life. Here are some highlights of each.

Amazing Earth #1: Our Milky Way is a benign galaxy. All major galaxies we have observed have supermassive black holes at their centers. Some of these monsters are more than 10 billion times as massive as our Sun. The black hole at the center of the Milky Way, Sagittarius A*, is "only" 4 million times our Sun's mass. This means Sag A* has consumed 1000 times fewer stars, gas, and the odd planet than black holes in other galaxies. It also means Sag A* has emitted 1000 times less deadly radiation. Our galaxy is more habitable with a smaller monster at its center.

Amazing Earth #2: We are in our galaxy's habitable zone. Even in a benign galaxy, astrobiologists estimate only 10% of our galaxy is habitable. Nearer the galaxy center, radiation levels are too hazardous. Farther from the center, gas densities are too low to support the formation of the massive stars that produce the atoms life needs — carbon, oxygen, iron, phosphorous, and many others.

Amazing Earth #3: Our Sun was born at the right time. The early epochs of our universe were hellish, punctuated by frequent cataclysmic collisions, explosions, and intense radiation. The universe is much more serene as of late (the last 6 billion years or so), and as the universe has expanded, many cosmic monsters have moved farther away.

Additionally, the early universe lacked the atoms that life requires. These atoms were slowly produced by billions of trillions of stars burning for billions of years. Our Sun was born after these atoms became sufficiently abundant.

Conversely, the gas clouds from which stars form have been depleted and dispersed over the eons. The star formation rate in our galaxy is now only about 10% of what it once was.

Our Solar System was born after most of the mayhem, after life's atoms became available, but before star-forming gas disappeared.

Amazing Earth #4: Our Sun is a lone star. Most stars have partners; they are part of multi-star systems. Almost any orbit can be stable for a planet near a single star, but almost no orbits are stable over the long-term for planets subject to strong gravity from two or more stars.

Amazing Earth #5: Our Sun is the right type of star. Our Sun and its planets formed from a gas cloud with a favorable composition, having a great abundance of the atoms life requires. Also, our Sun's mass is in the favorable range. More massive stars do not live long enough for life to develop on nearby planets. Less massive stars produce very little energy and are often quite unstable. These stars have very small habitable zones in their extreme proximity. Close-in planets are tidally-locked to their star, like our Moon is to Earth — one side always faces the star, while the other side is in eternal darkness.

On a tidally-locked planet, neither side can support life. Additionally, low-mass stars frequently emit intense flares of deadly radiation.

Amazing Earth #6: Water from the asteroid belt. Earth formed from the collisions and mergers of smaller rocky bodies. That process released an enormous amount of energy that melted our new-born planet through and through. Any initial water Earth had was lost — it vaporized, the hydrogen and oxygen dissociated, and the hydrogen floated out into space. When Earth eventually cooled, it was devoid of water. But all was not lost; water was not too far away.

Jupiter's gravitational tidal forces prevented a planet forming between it and Mars. The planetesimals that could not form a planet became the asteroid belt, which happens to be just beyond our Solar System's *snowline*, where water vapor condenses on solid bodies. The myriad asteroids have much greater surface area, and thus collect much more water, than would a single planet of the same total mass.

Planetary scientists believe that after the asteroid belt stabilized, Jupiter moved slightly closer to the Sun, thereby disrupting asteroid orbits. They estimate 99% of the original asteroids were sent plunging toward the Sun. Many of those asteroids struck Earth and delivered their water. We believe asteroids created our oceans and made Earth the Blue Planet.

Amazing Earth #7: We are protected by a big brother. The cosmos is full of lethal dangers. Periodically, objects from the outer Solar System and beyond plummet toward the Sun, pulled by its strong gravity. The giant planet Jupiter absorbs or deflects many such objects, thereby shielding Earth.

Amazing Earth #8: We are protected by a little sister. The Moon stabilizes the rotational axis of Earth, ensuring we have predictable, moderate seasons. As a percentage of its host planet, our Moon's mass is 50 times greater than any of the other 200 moons in our Solar System. None of those other moons has any appreciable effect on its host planet.

The rotational axes of some other planets, including Mars and Uranus, have changed over the eons, perhaps due to collisions or tidal gravitational forces. Uranus's north pole points nearly directly toward the Sun. If that happened to Earth, our oceans would evaporate in the Northern Hemisphere and freeze solid in the Southern Hemisphere.

Amazing Earth #9: The Sun's distance is optimal. Perhaps the most important factor in determining planetary habitability is *insolation*: how much light it receives from its star. Earth is in the middle of our Sun's habitable zone, where a planet's surface temperature allows water to exist in its liquid phase. Earth's average temperature is 58°F (15°C), which is very pleasant indeed.

Amazing Earth #10: Earth's orbit is nearly circular. Building on reason #9, having a favorable average temperature is nice, but life needs a survivable temperature year-round. Circular orbits provide that.

Some planetary orbits are more *eccentric* than others. Mercury is sometimes 50% farther from our Sun than at other times; its insolation varies by ±60%. And, some exoplanets are sometimes 10 times closer to their stars than at other times. Planets with highly eccentric orbits might go in and out of the habitable zone of their stars, imperiling any indigenous life.

We need not worry; Earth's distance from the Sun never varies by more than 1.7% (it is closest on January 3rd).

Amazing Earth #11: Earth's mass is optimal. The gravity of very massive planets is strong enough to prevent the escape of even the lightest gases, hydrogen and helium. Since those two gases account for 98% of all the atomic mass in the universe, giant planets are primarily comprised of gases incapable of supporting life.

Additionally, any solid or liquid surface that giant planets might have are deeply buried beneath immense hydrogen and helium atmospheres, which is also inhospitable.

Conversely, the gravity of small planets is insufficient to retain essential gases, such as water vapor. Earth's mass provides a gravitational force that retains the right gases, but not the wrong ones.

Amazing Earth #12: Earth's plate tectonics recycles carbon. Earth is the only planet we know that has plate tectonics, the continual recycling of land masses and ocean basins. Organic debris, from both living and dead plants and animals, collects at the bottom of our oceans. (Rivers carry terrestrial debris into the oceans). Carbon atoms in that debris would be forever lost to the ecosystem without plate tectonics.

Amazing Earth #13: Our magnetic field protects our atmosphere. Of all terrestrial planets, Earth has by far the strongest magnetic field. This field shields our atmosphere from the solar wind, a torrent of charged particles that would blast air molecules out into space.

We believe Mars once had an atmosphere and oceans full of water, but lost both because its magnetic field is much weaker than ours.

The remarkable strength of Earth's magnetic field is due in part to an unusually large amount of iron in its core, which also gives Earth the highest density of any major body in our Solar System.

It is suspected that much of Earth's iron came here when the nascent Earth was struck by another developing planet, in a cataclysmic collision that formed the Moon.

Amazing Earth #14: Earth's atmosphere supports life. We all have to breathe, and as far as we know, Earth is the only planet with a life-sustaining atmosphere. As an added bonus, our atmosphere is transparent to light, allowing us to look outward and enjoy the majesty of our universe.

I do not claim that life could not exist on a planet without all of these characteristics, but each is certainly very important in supporting life on Earth.

Now that we have some information on nearly 4000 planets outside our Solar System, we can estimate the odds of an average planet having half of the above characteristics. (For the other half, we have no information as of yet.) Those data show Earth may well be as special as 1 in a billion, or even more.

FINELY TUNED UNIVERSE

"What really interests me is
whether God had any choice in the
creation of the universe"

— Albert Einstein

I believe Einstein wondered whether the laws of nature allow universes that are very different from ours. In the half-century since Einstein died, we have discovered that vastly different universes are possible. In fact, vastly different universes may be much more probable. It seems that almost any other universe would most likely not support any form of life.

Science has discovered that our universe has just the right properties to support life in many ways that are extraordinarily improbable. Scientists have no naturalistic explanation for our good fortune; we call this "fine tuning."

Twenty characteristics of our universe, I call them "knobs", seem finely tuned. All the known laws of nature permit each knob to have any of a wide range of values, as illustrated by the gray band in Figure 3.

But, life of any form is possible only if each knob setting is within a very narrow range of values, the thin white bar near the arrow in Figure 3.

In our universe, each of the 20 knob settings is within the very narrow range that enables life. The universe could have been very different, we believe, but thankfully it is just right.

Let's explore a few examples.

Figure 3: One of 20 Knobs

Knob #1: The proton mass. All atoms are comprised of three particles: protons, neutrons, and electrons. Every electron in the universe is exactly identical to every other electron. Physicists cannot discover any intrinsic differences, but more importantly, neither can nature. Quantum mechanics shows that if nature recognized even the slightest difference, every atom in the universe would collapse. There would be no stars and no life. All protons are also identical, as are all neutrons.

If the proton mass were slightly greater (relative to the neutron mass), protons would decay and atoms would never form. If the proton mass were slightly less, stars would cease to burn. Either way, there would be no life.

Knob #2: An ideal carbon resonance. Living creatures produce many millions of types of molecules based on chains of carbon atoms, some of which are amazingly complex with billions of atoms. By contrast, nature spontaneously produces only about 10,000 types of molecules that do not contain carbon; all those are quite simple, a dozen atoms or less.

Life is complex, and it requires complex molecules to digest food, to build its structures, to replicate, and to store the information that specifies the recipes that ensure survival. Only carbon-based molecules can encode those recipes.

Carbon is produced only in stars by the fusion of three helium nuclei. This process is very difficult because three helium nuclei have much more energy than one carbon nucleus. That excess energy must be released before colliding helium nuclei fly apart.

But nuclear reactions happen much more rapidly than the electromagnetic reactions that can carry away the excess energy. Without a dramatic surprise, there would be almost no carbon in our universe, and therefore no life.

The dramatic surprise is: carbon has a *nuclear resonance* at just the right energy to match three helium nuclei. Nuclear resonances are like harmonics in music. Striking middle C on a piano produces sound at that base frequency plus softer tones at various multiples of that frequency. Physicists call those higher-frequency tones resonances. By analogy, nuclei have base states plus higher-energy resonance states.

Science cannot explain why the carbon resonance happens to perfectly match three helium nuclei, but only because it does is there carbon and life in our universe.

Knob #3: Antimatter. For every particle of matter, there is a corresponding particle of antimatter — the yin to matter's yang (see Figure 4). When a particle of matter meets its corresponding antimatter alter-ego, the two particles *annihilate*: the mass-energy of both particles is converted into radiation.

Figure 4: Matter and Antimatter

Annihilation leaves absolutely no trace that either particle ever existed.

There are very strong reasons to believe that when our universe was born, it contained exactly equal amounts of matter and antimatter. If it had remained that way, all particles would have annihilated one another within a few seconds, leaving nothing to form stars, planets, and life.

Fortunately, life is saved by a knob once again. While three of nature's four forces treat matter and antimatter identically, the weak nuclear force shows a tiny bit of favoritism. As my thesis experiment, and other experiments as well, showed, nature favors matter over antimatter by 50.15% to 49.85%. This is called CP-violation, and is truly bizarre — nature deviates from perfect symmetry by 0.3%. Figure 4 tries to portray this with a gray circle in the white yang, and a white circle in the black yin.

We actually don't know which type of particle nature favors. But, we choose to call ourselves "matter".

Due to this slight CP-asymmetry, by the time the universe was 1 second old, a very tiny excess of matter had developed. For every one billion particles of antimatter, there were one billion *and one* particles of matter. The two billions annihilated, each particle of antimatter taking one particle of matter into oblivion, leaving behind the extra one in a billion particle of matter.

If the CP-knob had a slightly higher or slightly lower value, our universe would never have formed stars, planets, and life.

Knob #4: Ideal cosmic expansion rate. The initial expansion rate of the universe, relative to its energy density, could have been almost anything.

Had the expansion rate been very slightly higher, the universe would have expanded too rapidly to form stars, atoms, and life.

Had the expansion rate been very slightly lower, the entire universe would have collapsed into a single black hole, without stars, atoms, or life.

The viable zone covers only 1 part in 100 trillion, trillion, trillion, trillion. Would you bet the farm on that?

The conclusion must be that science has precisely described an amazing mystery, but has not provided an answer.

Each of us may answer in our own way.

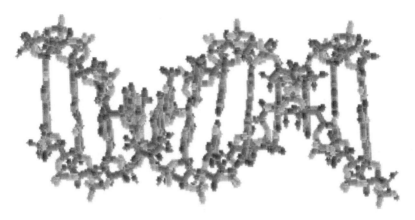

Figure 5: A short segment of DNA

DAZZLING DNA

The most spectacular object ever discovered by science is DNA, deoxyribonucleic acid, the genetic code of life. Each of our 10 trillion body cells contains a complete set of DNA, each with over 100 billion atoms.

One set of our DNA has about as many atoms as a typical galaxy has stars, but with one critical difference. Billions of stars on a galaxy's left side could be swapped with billions of stars on its right side, and the galaxy would continue spinning unfazed. But, exchanging even a few atoms in DNA could be fatal; there is remarkably little room for error.

The DNA of every creature studied so far has the same biochemical structure: a *double-helix*, a twisted ladder, with rails comprised of sugar molecules and rungs comprised of *nucleotide base-pairs*. A tiny snippet of DNA is shown in Figure 5.

All DNA we know uses the same four base-pairs (A, C, G, T) to direct the assembly of proteins from the same set of amino acids.

The four-letter code spells out a book of life. But these books are vastly larger than any written by man.

Your genetic code would fill 1500 volumes of an encyclopedia. Even the code of the humblest bacteria would come close to filling one volume.

Science really has no idea how such an intricate structure could have first originated.

Darwinian evolution provides an effective model for how species change gradually over many generations in response to environmental pressures. But, where did the first life come from?

Even in the most favorable possible scenario — with all the carbon in the observable universe, all in a perfect habitat, interacting at the highest possible rate since the instant of the Big Bang — spontaneously forming the DNA of just one organism is absurdly improbable, as discussed in Chapter 5.

DNA is the most complex, most sophisticated object we know. It's truly miraculous, even if its origin is entirely natural.

For more about DNA see Appendix D.

Science can indeed enrich faith.

Chapter 8

Science & Faith Are Compatible

"Science without religion is lame,
religion without science is blind"
— Albert Einstein

In this final chapter, let's explore the common ground between science and faith, and the value of mutually beneficial cooperation.

TWO DESCRIPTIONS OF CREATION

Some Dividers stress the differing views of the creation of our universe espoused by science and major religions.

The next two pages compare some highlights of two creation stories: the Big Bang theory and the Book of Genesis.

Both start with a startling statement: the universe did not always exist; it began in an instant at a specific moment in time.

The Big Bang theory addresses only what happened *after* the beginning; it does not describe *how* or *why* our universe began. Scientists have some speculations about *before* and *how*, but no comprehensive models.

Big Bang Theory

· Long ago, there was nothing

· Our universe began in an instant

· First came energy, space and time (light)

· Stars and galaxies

· Planets

· Plants and animals

· Humans

· All this took 13.8 billion years

Genesis describes the beginning unforgettably: "And God said let there be light."

The Big Bang theory says our universe began with the creation of space, time, and energy, which physicists would say is a reasonable description of light.

Both describe the creation of stars (heavenly firmament) and dry land (planets), followed by plant and animal life, and ultimately humans.

These two descriptions of creation come from greatly different philosophical foundations; they originated thousands of years apart, and at greatly different stages in the development of human societies.

I am amazed at how similar they are.

Book of Genesis

- Long ago, there was nothing

- God created the universe in an instant

- God said "Let there be light"

- Heavenly firmament

- Dry land (Earth)

- Plants and animals

- Humans

- All this took 6 days

On the last line, we do find a major discrepancy. Genesis says all this happened in 6 days, while the Big Bang theory says this took 13.8 billion years — a big difference. Each of us must decide the importance of the numbers versus the message. How much should we emphasize one large difference versus many similarities?

The Big Bang theory was first proposed by Georges Lemaître, a Belgian Catholic priest and professor of physics. See Appendix B for more about Big Bang cosmology.

In 1996, Pope John Paul II declared the Big Bang theory consistent with Catholic theology, albeit with the proviso that this occurred under the guidance of God.

BOOKS OF KNOWLEDGE

St. Augustine said God was the author of the Book of Scripture, as well as the Book of Nature. Since God created nature, he reasoned, we can learn about Him through everything we see.

The German astronomer, Johannes Kepler, said: "God wants to be known through the Book of Nature."

The Book of Nature is more ancient than the Book of Scripture, but before the advent of modern science, we were poor readers of the older Book. While the revelation of nature was delayed by human limitations, that does not diminish the value or validity of what we are now learning from the Book of Nature. We should not reject new knowledge simply because we failed to discover it earlier. After all, the Dead Sea Scrolls were discovered only 60 years ago; once authenticated, the Scrolls were accepted as an additional part of Scripture.

If humans weren't intended to continually learn more, why are we so good at it?

Rejecting knowledge from the Book of Nature is a poor strategy for promoting faith. When scientists discovered that the Sun, not Earth, was the center of our Solar System, religious leaders responded by burning "heretics" at the stake. That silenced scientists for a time, but even the most powerful cannot rewrite the Book of Nature. Centuries later, that response remains a stain of unreasoning inhumanity.

Pope John Paul II enunciated a much more effective strategy: seeking common understanding of the truth of nature and the truth of scripture.

Misrepresenting knowledge from the Book of Nature is also a poor strategy for promoting science. Nature will ultimately expose the dishonesty of anyone attempting to misrepresent its truth.

THE OLDEST TESTAMENT

Continuing the concept of the Book of Nature, Figure 6 shows its "Oldest Testament", an image of the Cosmic Microwave Background (CMB) radiation that predates the Torah, the New Testament, and the Koran by more than 13 billion years.

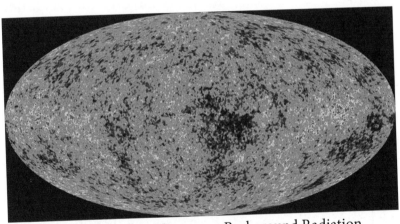

Figure 6: Cosmic Microwave Background Radiation

Figure 6 is an actual photograph, taken by NASA's WMAP satellite, of our universe just 380,000 years after its beginning.

The microwave "light" we see today has just reached Earth after traveling for nearly 14 billion years from the farthest reaches of our observable universe.

The CMB light carried with it, as if in a time capsule, this image of what the universe looked like at nearly the dawn of time.

The CMB is the oldest data, artifact, relic, or text that mankind will ever discover. If we compare the universe today to a 100-year-old person, this would be their sonogram 24 hours after the moment of conception. Each small white dot in this image has expanded over billions of years to become a cluster of galaxies.

How can we "read" this Oldest Testament? Some scholars are experts in reading Aramaic, and others are experts in reading scientific data. Scientists can decipher this data as surely as anyone can decipher ancient texts.

Several images like this one have been processed mathematically to find their *power spectrum*, a quantitative measure of how "clumpy" the images are. A power spectrum of an oil painting would tell us what brush sizes the artist used and how often he used each size. The CMB power spectrum shown in Figure 7 describes the "brush sizes" employed in the creation of the universe.

The dots in Figure 7 represent the measured data; the vertical bars indicate their precision limits. The curve, from our best Big Bang theory of cosmology, matches the data extremely well, providing strong confirmation of this model.

The match reveals the age of the universe, 13.8 ± 0.06 billion years, and tells us much more.

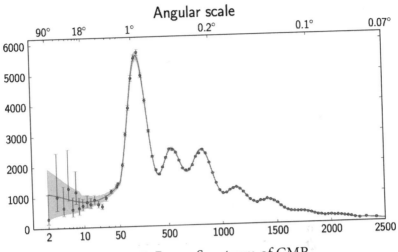

Figure 7: Power Spectrum of CMB

The CMB is the most perfect *black body* radiation ever observed, which means it comes entirely from heat energy rather than any effect of the color of the object that emitted the radiation.

When the universe was young, it was very hot. So, the energy of the CMB radiation when it was emitted was quite high. Since then, the universe has greatly expanded, and the CMB we observe today has much less energy — its average energy corresponds to a temperature of -455°F.

Some erroneously claim this disproves the Big Bang theory. They claim the change in CMB energy violates a cherished principle of physics: the conservation of energy.

The truth is: the CMB provides strong evidence of the Big Bang theory, and it has conserved energy. As explained further in Appendix C, energy is conserved in a constant frame of reference. In any such frame, the CMB's energy has never changed.

SPIRITUAL AND PRACTICAL KNOWLEDGE

Consider human knowledge falling into two broad categories: spiritual and practical. Practical knowledge covers our day-to-day activities and interactions with the material world. Spiritual knowledge relates to God, morality, love, kindness, charity, hope, and the purpose of our lives.

Spiritual knowledge addresses issues that have confronted mankind for as long as we have existed. These issues change modestly and slowly over the ages. Faith is the primary source of spiritual knowledge for most people.

Conversely, practical knowledge changes continually, rapidly, and dramatically. Agriculture has been part of practical knowledge for many thousand years, but that knowledge is enormously different today than it was in biblical times.

Other areas of practical knowledge have emerged only in the last 100 years, or even the last 10 years. These include building airplanes, sending rovers to Mars, reading ebooks on your tablet, and analyzing curved spacetime near the event horizon of a black hole. Very little practical knowledge from biblical times is still useful today.

While practical knowledge is sometimes used to illustrate its message, the objective of Scripture is spiritual, not practical, instruction. Scripture doesn't provide guidance on driving cars or performing open-heart surgery. Our best source of practical knowledge is science, which ultimately comes from the Book of Nature.

TWO POINTS OF VIEW

Science and faith can combine to benefit society more than either can separately.

Consider an analogy: binocular vision, as shown in Figure 8.

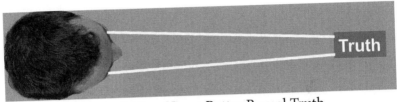

Figure 8. Two Views Better Reveal Truth

Our two eyes provide two slightly different views — if our eyes saw exactly the same thing, we wouldn't need two eyes. Neither view is "wrong", but neither sees everything — try looking at your surroundings with one eye shut.

We see more and can better understand our world with two eyes. In fact, it is the *difference* between our two views that provides depth perception.

If we intelligently combine two complimentary perspectives — science and faith — we will better perceive Truth, something we all seek.

Those instances in which science and faith have worked together have been very productive.

Religious groups have founded many great universities that have educated countless excellent students, including scientists.

Similarly, religious groups have founded many great hospitals. People of faith, inspired by their beliefs, have invested their time and money to help others.

They've built world-class medical centers that provide the latest pharmaceuticals, the most modern scientific equipment, and the most scientifically knowledgeable medical staff. Countless lives have been saved as a result.

Instead of walls, let's build more hospitals together.

Appendix A

ATOMS

In the first of his famed *Lectures on Physics,* Nobel Laureate Richard Feynman said the most important discovery of science was:

"All things are made of atoms."

This discovery did not come easily.

PROVING ATOMS EXIST

For 25 centuries, mankind debated what matter was ultimately made of — if we cut something into smaller and smaller pieces, will we ever reach an "end", or can we keeping cutting it into ever smaller pieces forever?

This quandary can be restated: is matter continuous, or is it comprised of small discrete parts that somehow link together.

The two alternatives are illustrated in Figure A-1.

In the 5th century B.C., the Greek natural philosopher Democritus argued that matter is discrete. He is credited with being the first person to name these smallest parts of matter, calling them *atomos,* a Greek word meaning uncuttable.

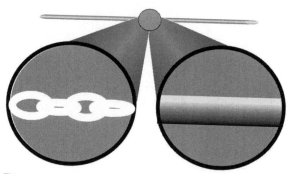

Figure A-1: Is Matter Discrete or Continuous?

In Figure A-1, a thin wire runs along at the top of the image. We examine the wire using high-magnification binoculars. If matter is continuous, we would see the image on the right. But if matter is made of discrete parts, at sufficient magnification, we would see the left image.

Unfortunately, for millennia no one had an instrument sensitive enough to detect atoms. Absent observational evidence, the philosophical debate continued into the 20th century. By then, many had grown tired of the unsubstantiated belief in the existence of atoms, and many leading physicists strongly argued against them.

In 1827, English Botanist Robert Brown used a microscope to examine tiny pollen grains suspended in a liquid. He saw the pollen grains moving erratically and mysteriously, darting one way and then suddenly changing direction with no apparent cause. For most of a century, no one was able to explain the mystery of *Brownian motion.*

Then in 1905, Albert Einstein claimed Brownian motion was due to the pollen grains being continually struck by the liquid's atoms, which were too small to be seen with a normal microscope. Einstein

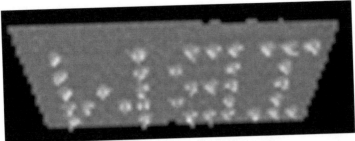

Figure A-2: Atoms on a Nickel Plate

derived a *diffusion* equation that predicts how rapidly an average pollen grain moves through the liquid, depending on the mass of the liquid's atoms. When precise experiments confirmed Einstein's predictions, the atomic hypothesis — that everything is made of atoms — became universally accepted.

Much more advanced modern "microscopes" that do not employ visible light can "image" individual atoms, as shown in Figure A-2. This image was made by an atomic force microscope in the central research labs of a major international corporation.

After 25 centuries, Democritus was finally proven right: matter is comprised of tiny pieces that are uncuttable. But what we choose to call atoms are actually easily "cut", and their parts can be cut one more time.

We now know that atoms are comprised of electrons, protons, and neutrons, while protons and neutrons are comprised of quarks. And that is where it stops, we believe.

We believe electrons, quarks, and some other particles are *elementary* — not made of anything else — they are indeed uncuttable.

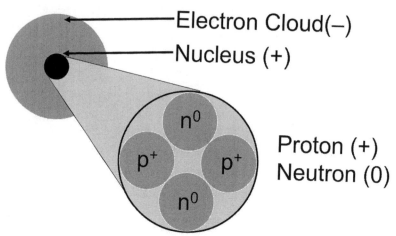

Figure A-3: Parts of an Atom and its Nucleus

Perhaps we employed Democritus' word *atomos* too soon. If we had waited another half-century, we may have saved "atoms" for truly uncuttable particles, like electrons and quarks.

INSIDE AN ATOM

As sketched in Figure A-3, atoms have two main parts: a nucleus that is surrounded by a cloud of electrons. Nuclei are typically 100,000 times smaller than the electron clouds surrounding them, but they are much more massive, up to 4000 times as massive as their electrons.

Atomic nuclei have positive electric charges, and electrons have negative electric charges. Opposite polarity charges attract one another, which is what holds atoms together — that is a good thing.

An atom's nucleus is comprised of protons that have a positive charge and neutrons with zero charge.

Electric charges of the same polarity repel one another, which makes one wonder why nuclei with multiple protons don't fall apart.

The answer is: all combinations of protons and neutrons attract one another with the strong nuclear force. As its name suggests, the strong force is about 100 times stronger than the electric force.

While the electric force pushes protons apart, the strong force pulls them together.

For the most common nuclei, the strong force dominates, making the nuclei stable. But, for nuclei with too many protons, the electric force eventually wins, and the nuclei *decay*, falling apart into smaller pieces. Uranium has the largest stable nucleus, with 92 protons.

ATOMS ARE FOREVER

Some types of atoms are unstable — they decay. Such atoms are generally quite rare — a few in every billion atoms.

The vast majority of atoms are stable — they may indeed endure forever, longer than stars, galaxies, and perhaps even the universe as we know it.

This is because, in most cases, there is only one way for an atom's parts to "fit together".

A hydrogen atom created just after the Big Bang, as almost all were, is still brand new, in precisely the same condition as it was nearly 14 billion years ago.

There is no way to "scratch" an atom, and no way an atom can become "wrinkled". Atoms cannot bear "scars", and none of their parts ever wear out.

Atoms cannot age — they are eternal.

TYPES OF ATOMS

The number of protons in an atom's nucleus determines its *element number* and all of its primary properties. In electrically neutral atoms, the number of electrons equals the number of protons.

Some common elements are listed in the table on the next page.

In the universe overall, hydrogen and helium, the elements made shortly after the Big Bang, account for 98% of all atomic mass and 99% of all atoms.

The major elements of life amount to only 2% of the universe's atomic mass.

Indeed, life is comprised of rare ingredients. Hydrogen accounts for only 10% of our body mass, and we have no helium at all. Instead, 65% of our body mass is oxygen and 18% is carbon.

For those who might think that tiny particles can't make much difference on our much grander scale, consider that gold and lead differ by just 3 protons.

As we will discuss later, a substantial change in one's DNA can be effected by moving a single proton.

Element	#p	#n	%U	%H
Hydrogen	1	0	74	10
Helium	2	2	24	0
Carbon	6	6	0.5	18
Oxygen	8	8	1.0	65
Iron	26	30	0.1	<0.05
Gold	79	118	2*	140*
Lead	82	126	27*	1700*
Uranium	92	146	0.3*	130*

This table lists the most common form of various elements. Here, #p denotes the number of protons, #n denotes the number of neutrons, %U denotes the percentage by mass of that element relative to the mass of all atoms averaged throughout the universe, %H denotes the mass percent of that element in humans, and * denotes parts per billion rather than %.

ATOMIC FINGERPRINTS IN LIGHT

Atoms have an amazing property that is vital to our understanding of the universe.

Each type of atom absorbs and emits a specific set of wavelengths of light — a unique *spectrum* — a "fingerprint" that is easily distinguished from that of any other type of atom.

This enables astronomers to analyze the chemical composition of all the stars and other luminous objects in the heavens simply by examining their light.

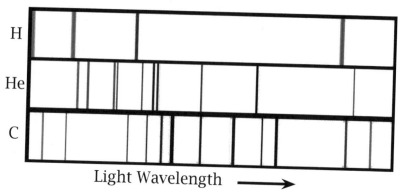

Figure A-4: Spectra of Three Types of Atoms

The spectra of hydrogen, helium, and carbon are illustrated in Figure A-4. Each vertical line represents a wavelength that type of atom emits or absorbs.

Additionally, when light sources move toward or away from us, these spectra shift slightly due to the Doppler effect. When light sources move away from us, their spectra are *redshifted*, increasing their wavelengths; when they move toward us, their spectra are *blueshifted*, decreasing their wavelengths.

By measuring these shifts, astronomers can precisely determine the speed of any visible object. This capability enabled the discovery that the universe is expanding, and that it had a beginning, as we explore in Appendix B.

Appendix B

Big Bang Cosmology

LEMAITRE'S PRIMEVAL ATOM

The first suggestions that the universe might be expanding, and might have begun from something extremely small, came from Georges Lemaître, a Belgian Catholic priest and professor of physics at the Catholic University of Leuven.

In 1927, Lemaître published his idea that the universe was expanding. Unfortunately, his work appeared in a journal that was not widely read outside Belgium. It received little attention for several years.

Gradually, Lemaître became better known in scientific circles. In 1931, he published a paper claiming the universe originated from a single point that he called the "Primeval Atom".

Einstein is said to have told Lemaître something like: your mathematics may be correct, but your physics is abominable. Einstein, like most scientists and the general public, then strongly clung to the belief that the universe always was and always will be as we see it now.

The name "Big Bang" came much later. British physicist Sir Fred Hoyle espoused the Steady State theory, a competing vision of the universe.

In a 1949 radio show, he characterized his opponents' theory, perhaps derisively, saying it claimed everything came out of a "big bang". Whatever Hoyle's intentions, the name stuck, and became a cherished moniker.

LEAVITT'S CEPHEID RULE

Scientific evidence for the Big Bang theory of cosmology slowly developed in the early 20th Century, as astronomers gradually learned how to solve their greatest challenge: measuring the distance to the stars.

For centuries, astronomers struggled to estimate the size of the heavens. They developed over 30 different techniques, none of which provided more than crude guesses.

The first major advance was due to Henrietta Swan Leavitt. In 1912, Leavitt discovered a simple relationship between the period and luminosity of Cepheid *variable stars.*

Variable stars brighten and dim in regularly repeating cycles; each full cycle is called one period. Some variables are actually two nearby stars that orbit one another, with one star occasionally eclipsing its partner. Other variable stars pulsate — alternately expanding and becoming brighter, and later contracting and becoming dimmer.

Cepheid variables are extremely bright, from 300 to 30,000 times more luminous than our Sun. This is very advantageous — astronomers can find Cepheids even in remote galaxies.

According to Leavitt's rule, two Cepheid variables with the same period have the same intrinsic peak brightness — both stars emit the same amount of light at the maximum of their cycles. If one appears to us to be dimmer, it must be because it is farther from Earth.

HUBBLE DISCOVERS EXPANSION

The next step occurred when Edwin Hubble found Cepheid variables in several "spiral nebulae". At that time, our Milky Way galaxy was thought to be the entire universe, and these "nebulae" were thought to be clouds of gas and dust.

Employing Leavitt's rule, Hubble discovered that these "nebulae" were actually 100 times farther away than any previously known objects.

To be that far and appear as bright as they were, these "nebulae" had to contain billions of stars. They weren't nebulae at all — they had to be galaxies of their own, far beyond the reaches of our own galaxy.

Hubble then measured the *redshifts* of these galaxies, which determined how fast the galaxies were moving toward or away from us. (See Appendix A.)

Comparing galaxy distances to their redshifts, Hubble announced in 1929 the greatest astronomical discovery of the 20th Century.

To understand this fully, imagine taking the measured distances and speeds of many galaxies, and plotting that data, as shown in Figure B-1.

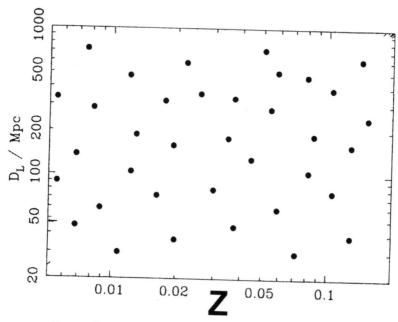

Figure B-1: Possible Plot of Distance vs. Redshift

Here, each dot represents one galaxy, with its distance plotted vertically and its speed (redshift z) plotted horizontally.

At first, we might expect what this plot shows: dots scattered throughout the chart, showing no obvious relationship between distance and speed.

After all, why should the two be related?

Indeed, the universe *could* very well have been like Figure B-1.

But it isn't.

What Hubble actually found is plotted in Figure B-2 — all the galaxies in the plot fall on a straight line.

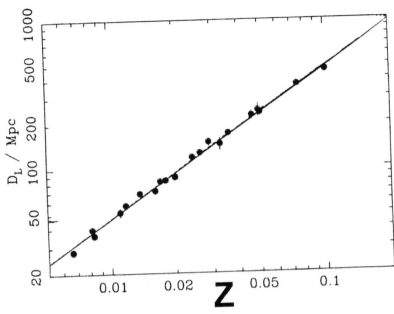

Figure B-2: Hubble's Law

Hubble found that all remote galaxies are moving away from us, and all are moving according to another simple rule.

The rule, called Hubble's law, says: every celestial object is moving away at a speed that is proportional to its distance.

So, if galaxy A is 15 times farther from us than galaxy B, A will be moving away from us 15 times faster than B.

We observe this is true, but how can this happen? Why are all remote galaxies moving away from us? How does each galaxy in the universe "know" how fast to move?

What coordinates all this motion so precisely?

EINSTEIN'S SPACETIME

Einstein's theory of general relativity says space is flexible and dynamic — space can curve, twist, and stretch. Relativity says no *thing* can move through space faster than light, but *space* can change at any speed.

So, galaxies are not really moving through space, each in exactly the right direction, at just exactly the right speed — it is space itself that is changing. Space is expanding uniformly in all three dimensions, and as it does, it carries galaxies along with it.

Expanding space provides the choreography that ensures all galaxies move properly.

To understand this better, imagine a rubber strip to which buttons have been sewn, as shown in Figure B-3.

As we stretch the rubber more and more (image bottom to top), the buttons move apart. From the "viewpoint" of each button, all other buttons are moving away from it. Buttons that are twice as far apart are separating twice as fast, just because there

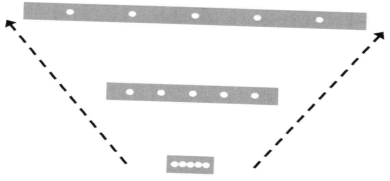

Figure B-3: Buttons Sewn on Rubber Strip

is twice as much rubber stretching between them. The buttons move according to Hubble's law.

By analogy, galaxies are moving apart in precise accord with Hubble's law because every part of space is expanding in all three dimensions at the same rate.

HUBBLE'S LAW IMPLIES A BEGINNING

Imagine being atop the Seattle Space Needle looking through a telescope at traffic leaving town for a three-day weekend.

Now, suppose we observe that all vehicles on the freeway are moving according to Hubble's law, as shown in Figure B-4. The minivan is 100 miles away doing 25 miles per hour (mph), while the sports car is twice as far away going twice as fast.

Imagine we have a video recording of all this traffic, and we play it backwards. The minivan would then be moving backwards toward the Space Needle at 25 mph, and would arrive in 4 hours. The sports car would be moving backwards toward the Space Needle at 50 mph, and would also arrive in 4 hours.

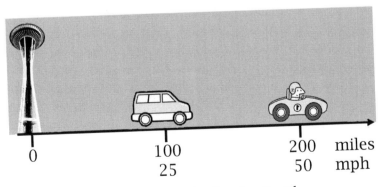

Figure B-4: Vehicles Leaving Seattle

In fact, every vehicle on the freeway would arrive back at the Space Needle in the same 4 hours, simply because every vehicle's speed is proportional to its distance per Hubble's law.

This means, 4 hours before the scene in Figure B-4, all vehicles were in the same place at the same time.

By analogy, since everything in the universe is moving in accordance with Hubble's law — being carried by uniformly expanding space — all galaxies must have once been in the same place at the same time.

That place and time was the Big Bang.

UNIVERSAL EXPANSION EQUATION

Einstein's theory of general relativity links energy density with the geometry of spacetime. This has the remarkable consequence that, for our universe, there is only one solution to Einstein's equations.

In Newton's theory of gravity, there are an infinite number of ways that our universe could have become what we see today. But, we now know that Newton's laws are not the proper description of nature — our universe evolves according to general relativity.

Because of the properties of our universe, as measured with the CMB (cosmic microwave background radiation, see Appendix C), Einstein's equations have only one solution for the expansion of the universe:

$$3\,H^2 = 8\pi\,\varepsilon$$

Here, H is the Hubble expansion rate, and ε is the energy density. Considering this equation describes the entire universe, it is remarkably simple.

We can measure the values of H and ε today, which allows us to calculate how the universe will evolve as time marches forward. But perhaps more importantly, we can also calculate how the universe evolved in the past.

The equations of physics do not tell us how things *are now* — we have to measure that — rather the equations tell us how things *change* in both directions of time.

With measurements of how things (H and ε) are now and Einstein's equations for how things change, we can calculate the global conditions of the universe (including size and temperature) nearly all the way back to the beginning of time.

We can confidently state what our universe was like all the way back to a trillionth of a trillionth of 1 second. Some might say much earlier than that.

One vital conclusion emerges from all this analysis: our universe has always been expanding and will continue to expand forever. It will never stop expanding and start collapsing.

Physicists once wondered if a collapsing phase was possible. If so, that might have ended in a Big Crunch, everything collapsing into a single point — ending as it started.

Some thought a Big Crunch might ignite another Big Bang, and that this cycle of expansion, collapse, expansion, ... might continue forever into the future as well as forever into the past.

Assuming the global geometry of our universe is Euclidean, as the CMB analysis shows, such reversals will never happen.

The righthand side of the expansion equation must always be greater than zero, because as little as one particle makes the energy density greater than zero.

This means the lefthand side of the expansion equation can never be zero, and therefore H, the expansion rate, can never be zero.

Any reversal — expansion-to-contraction or contraction-to-expansion — requires that H pass through zero. Since H can never be zero, there can never be such a reversal, and since we observe that H is now greater than zero, our universe must always have been, and always will be, expanding.

As in all descriptions of nature, there are many complex and intriguing details to this story, but the this Appendix provides the essential ideas of Big Bang cosmology, our best model of our universe.

Appendix C

CMB — Evidence for Big Bang

In the beginning, our universe was a fireball — a ball of extraordinarily hot gas comprised of elementary particles. As thermodynamics explains, all gases cool as they expand. (This is how a refrigerator works.)

We discovered in Appendix B, that our universe has continually expanded since its beginning, and will expand forever. As it expands, it also cools.

We estimate that, by the time the universe was 1 second old, its temperature had dropped all the way down to 10 billion K, about 18 billion °F. This is too cold to create new particles, but much too hot for atoms to form — protons and electrons had so much heat energy that they bounced off one another rather than sticking together.

A gas of charged particles, called a *plasma*, very effectively absorbs light of all frequencies. This is why we cannot see through a flame — the fire's heat ionizes air molecules, ripping some electrons out of their atoms, creating plasma.

The plasma in our fireball universe effectively trapped light, continually absorbing and re-emitting every photon of light.

That changed when the universe became 380,000 years old, and its temperature was about 3000 K.

At 3000 K, about 6000°F, the universe was cool enough for protons and electrons to stick together and form the first atoms.

The electric charges of protons and electrons are equal in magnitude and opposite in polarity — protons have positive charge, electrons have negative charge, and a hydrogen atom with one of each has zero net charge.

Neutral atoms absorb only a tiny fraction of any particles of light that strike them. A gas of neutral atoms, such as Earth's atmosphere, is transparent.

Hence, for the first time in its history, our universe became transparent. The light of the universe, which had been trapped, could now propagate freely, as it has from that time onwards.

This first light is the CMB, the cosmic microwave background radiation, shown in Chapter 8, Figure 6.

The CMB is the afterglow of the primordial fireball that was our early universe. It shows us what the universe was like 380,000 years after the Big Bang.

We will certainly never have any earlier image of our universe using any form of light (electromagnetic radiation), since earlier light was trapped.

There is a remote possibility that we may one day be able to observe gravitational waves created at the instant of the Big Bang. But technical challenges make this extremely improbable.

In all likelihood, the CMB is the earliest image of our universe, in any form, that we will ever have.

While the CMB image might not make it onto your mantelpiece, it is in fact enormously informative. The CMB power spectrum shown in Chapter 8, Figure 7, has a dozen peaks and valleys, whose heights and widths reveal nature's deepest secrets.

Chapter 8 discusses fitting the prediction of the Big Bang theory to the CMB power spectrum.

This fit yields the age of the universe, 13.8 billion years, with a precision of 0.4% (± 0.06 billion years).

The fit also shows that the overall geometry of our universe is Euclidean (zero global spacetime curvature), with the same 0.4% precision.

The CMB image itself shows that, on a large scale, our universe was homogeneous (the same everywhere) to 1 part in 100,000, when it was 380,000 years old.

The temperature of CMB radiation that we observe on Earth today, is 2.725 K, 1090 times less than its temperature at the time and in the reference frame in which it was emitted. As discussed further below, the expansion of the universe stretches the wavelength of all light and changes our reference frame.

This temperature difference results from the expansion of the universe. Between the time the CMB was emitted and now, the universe has expanded in all three dimensions by a factor of 1090.

FOOTNOTE ON CMB

The CMB is the afterglow of the Big Bang. When this light was emitted, its energy was 1090 times higher than what we perceive today. Some individuals, including a few less-knowledgeable scientists, erroneously claim this apparent energy reduction violates the principle of energy conservation, thus invalidating the Big Bang theory. Those who understand Einstein's theory of relativity realize the fallacy of that claim.

Energy is definable only relative to an observer's reference frame. Cars on the opposite side of a highway seem to us to be moving much faster and have greater energy than those moving with us. If we make a U-turn, it would appear to us that the speed and energy of every other car changed, but of course that didn't happen. Each of our two differing perceptions is correct, but only within its own reference frame.

Energy is conserved only within an unchanging reference frame. The CMB light has exactly the same higher energy today as it did nearly 14 billion years ago, when measured in the reference frame in which it was emitted. The CMB also has the same lower energy today as it did back then, when measured in the reference frame we now inhabit.

The truth is: energy is conserved, and the CMB provides compelling evidence of the Big Bang 13.8 billion years ago.

Appendix D

DNA

Scientists are convinced that all forms of life on Earth have a common origin because all life on Earth is based on the same biochemical foundation.

All organisms eat, grow, and reproduce using basically the same proteins, made of the same amino acids, under the orchestration of genetic codes written in the same language: DNA, deoxyribonucleic acid.

DNA is a complex molecule that encodes not only all the biochemical processes necessary to sustain life, but also encodes the "blueprints" for building every cell in the body and for properly assembling those cells to create the whole living organism. The DNA in every living thing on Earth uses the same code to create proteins — a flower could make every human protein if it were reading our DNA instead of its own.

A physical model of a DNA segment is shown in Chapter 7, Figure 5. DNA has a double-helix structure comprised of two outer strands twisting around one another, with rungs connecting the outer strands. Each rung is a *base pair*, a combination of two matching *nucleotides* that are the elemental units of DNA. An entire set of DNA is replicated identically in virtually every cell throughout each organism's body.

DNA is huge by molecular standards — a single set of human DNA, from a single cell, could span five feet while being only one ten-millionth of an inch wide. One set of human DNA contains 3.2 billion base pairs and weighs a trillion times as much as a single hydrogen atom. There are as many atoms in one set of our DNA as there are stars in an average galaxy.

About 2% of human DNA is devoted to 22,000 individual *genes* that determine how to build the proteins that are essential to all body functions. The other 98% of our DNA was once called "junk" DNA, but we are learning that it too may have critical roles, such as regulating the activity of our genes.

Genes average 3000 base pairs, but that varies enormously. The gene responsible for muscle protein dystrophin has 2.5 million base pairs.

Surprisingly, neither the total amount of DNA nor the number of genes is a direct measure of how "advanced" an organism is. The amount of DNA in humans is not radically different from that of many other species that have a large number of body cells. And the DNA of some plants is much longer than ours.

The hepatitis B virus has the shortest known DNA at 3200 base pairs, and the DNA of some "nanobes" are not much larger. But these are not self-sustaining organisms; they are parasitic, relying on larger organisms for vital proteins they cannot produce.

Among self-sustaining organisms, the shortest known DNA has 460,000 base pairs, as reported by the Minimal Genome Project. This is roughly 7000 times smaller than human DNA.

Every form of life on Earth that has been studied so far has DNA base pairs comprised of four types of nucleotides, labeled A, C, G, and T. Thus, all genetic codes on Earth are written in the same four-letter alphabet. Every three base pairs functions as a unit called a *codon* that selects one of about 20 amino acids in the resulting protein or signals that the protein is complete.

The information storage capacity of DNA is truly mind-boggling. Twelve base pairs, four codons, can encode about 200,000 possible amino acid combinations. The number of amino acid combinations that the DNA of the simplest life form can encode is a 1 followed by 203,622 zeros!

The largest number I know that has any physical meaning is the number of photons in our observable universe: 1 followed by 89 zeros. We would have to multiply the number of photons times itself over 2000 times to approach the number of DNA combinations in even the simplest life.

Changes in DNA, called *mutations*, seem to occur randomly at a very low rate. In humans, the mutation rate in protein-coding genes is only one to two base pairs per generation. That works out to one base pair change per 50 million base pairs per generation. DNA replication achieves this astonishing fidelity because we have error-correcting processes that include comparing the two strands of our double-helix.

"Junk" and redundant DNA may play a surprisingly important role regarding mutations.

If a protein is defined by a gene that occurs only once, a mutation in that gene may very well disable it, with fatal consequences.

But a mutation in an extra copy of a gene or in the "junk" DNA is likely to have very little impact.

"Junk" and redundant DNA also provide an arena for safely "experimenting" with mutations. The eventual accumulation of many mutations may ultimately produce something useful. Having a lot of "junk" DNA substantially enhances the opportunity for developing useful mutations.

Figure D-1 shows a 4-base-pair segment of DNA, and the atomic composition of the four nucleotide base pairs: Adenine, Thymine, Guanine, and Cytosine. Adenine (A) always pairs with Thymine (T), and Cytosine (C) always pairs with Guanine (G).

The left strand in Figure D-1 reads (from top to bottom) ACTG, while the right strand reads the complement: TGAC.

Moving a single proton in Adenine changes it to its *tautomer* g, which is not identical to Guanine, but close enough that g bonds with Cytosine instead of Thymine.

This shows how sensitive DNA can be to errors — even the smallest change can effect a mutation.

Many other organic molecules also have similar tautometric mutations.

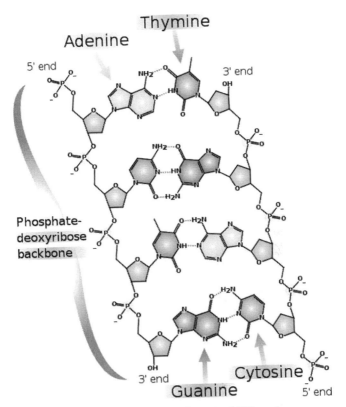

Figure D-1. DNA Chemical Diagram

Appendix F

Fusion in Stars

As discussed in Chapter 7, stars are essential in enabling life. Here, we explore in more detail how stars produce the energy and the atoms life requires through the process of nuclear fusion, the merging of smaller atomic nuclei to form larger ones.

FUSION PRODUCES ENERGY

As an energy source, nuclear fusion is 15 million times more efficient than burning gasoline, and fusion is clean. Fusion emits zero toxic waste, zero greenhouse gases, zero pollution, and no radioactive by-products.

Fusion is nature's way of making energy, and is the process that powers all the stars in the universe, including our favorite star: the Sun.

If the Sun had been comprised entirely of gasoline, burning as bright as it does, it would have burned out in less than 1000 years, far too little time for life to evolve on a nearby Blue Planet.

Fusing 1000 tons of hydrogen each year would power the needs of everyone on Earth — if only we could make nuclear fusion a practical reality.

Some day, I believe, mankind will be able to do just that.

Producing energy through nuclear fusion would solve many of humanity's critical problems, would greatly enrich everyone's life, and would eliminate the enormous costs and hazardous practices we now endure.

People have been working to develop fusion technology for many decades, but success remains elusive. For now, fusion is only in our stars.

THE NATURE OF NUCLEI

Nuclear fusion in stars is also the only source of life's essential ingredients: carbon, oxygen, and every other element except hydrogen.

The next section explores how stars make these essential atoms.

In this section, we explore the physics of nuclei, which some readers may choose to skip.

Nuclei consist of protons and neutrons. All combinations of these particles attract one another through the strong nuclear force. Protons, however, repel one another through the electric force. These competing forces leave some nuclei tightly bound, some weakly bound, and others unstable. The latter eventually decay, falling apart into smaller pieces.

The smallest and most ubiquitous nucleus is a single proton, the nucleus of normal hydrogen. This is the primary constituent of stars.

Beyond hydrogen, most common nuclei have equal numbers of protons and neutrons, and are tightly bound. These nuclei include carbon, nitrogen, and oxygen.

As nuclei become heavier, the number of neutrons generally exceeds the number of protons. The largest stable nucleus is uranium-238, with 92 protons and 146 neutrons.

The neutron excess and the instability of heavy nuclei are both due to protons repelling protons.

The range of the electric force is unlimited. Its strength decreases as the separation between electric charges increases, but it never drops to zero.

The strong force is about 100 times stronger than the electric force, but has a very limited range. Two protons separated by more than one proton diameter (1 trillionth of a millimeter) exert no strong force upon one another. The same applies to two neutrons, or a proton and a neutron.

Hence, in uranium, 92 protons repel one another with the electric force, which amounts to $92*91/2 = 4186$ repulsive forces. Conversely, only neighboring particles attract one another with the strong force, which amounts to roughly $92*6/2 = 276$ attractive forces.

The upshot of all this is: medium-sized nuclei are the most tightly bound. Small nuclei are less tightly bound, because they have fewer particles attracting one another with the strong force. Large nuclei are less tightly bound, because they have more protons repelling one another with the electric force.

The most tightly bound nucleus is iron-56.

Nature always seeks to reduce the energy of any system and convert the energy reduction into light or heat.

Reactions that make nuclear particles more tightly bound release energy and proceed vigorously. Reactions that make nuclear particles less tightly bound require something else to supply energy, severely disfavoring such reactions.

HOW STARS MAKE ATOMS

Nuclear fusion in stars proceeds in cycles. The first cycle is hydrogen fusion.

As a gas cloud collapses under its self-gravity, its core temperature rises. If the core becomes hot enough to ignite hydrogen fusion, a star is born.

Hydrogen fusing to create helium releases more energy than any other fusion process. Additionally, hydrogen is the most abundant nucleus. These two facts mean hydrogen fusion is every star's primary energy source, providing long-term stability for most of a star's existence.

Helium is heavier than hydrogen and accumulates in the star's core (the gravitational center), pushing hydrogen outwards.

Eventually, hydrogen is depleted in the core and the hydrogen fusion cycle wanes. The core pressure drops, allowing gravity to compress the core, thereby increasing its temperature. When the core becomes hot enough, the next fusion cycle starts: helium fusing to create carbon.

Helium fusion is the most critical step in producing the atoms of life. As explained by quantum mechanics, helium nuclei are more tightly bound than other light nuclei. Perhaps surprisingly, this results in there being no stable nucleus of eight particles — eight nuclear particles can minimize their total energy by splitting into two helium nuclei.

Hence, carbon production requires three helium nuclei to collide virtually simultaneously and stick together. The rarity of three body collisions is one impediment to carbon production.

Another impediment to carbon production, explored as Knob #2 in Chapter 7, is the release of excess energy: three helium nuclei have more energy than the stable nucleus of carbon. Serendipitously, carbon has a higher-energy resonant state that exactly matches the three-helium energy. The lifetime of the resonant state is long enough to allow the excess energy to be emitted as light.

Without this resonant state, our universe would have almost no carbon or any heavier elements.

As fusion proceeds, carbon accumulates in the star's core and pushes out the lighter nuclei, helium and hydrogen. The core pressure drops, gravity compresses the core and raises its temperature, eventually igniting carbon fusing to create oxygen.

Fusion cycles can continue through the production of iron-56, which is the most tightly bound nucleus. After iron, further fusion consumes energy rather than releasing it.

Only the most massive stars proceed through all the fusion cycles to iron.

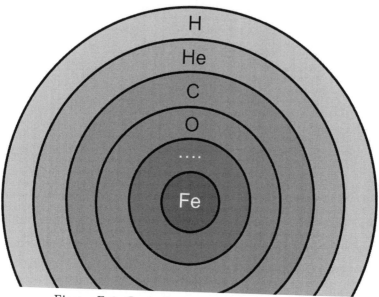

Figure F-1: Cross Section of End-Stage Star

Each cycle requires a higher core temperature, which creates a higher core pressure that the star's gravity must overcome.

The least massive stars never get past hydrogen fusion. Somewhat more massive stars stop at helium fusion. This trend continues: each successive fusion cycle requires an increased stellar mass. The most massive stars complete the production of iron, where fusion ends.

A massive end-stage star is comprised of layers: light elements near its surface and heavy elements near its core. In cross section, it looks a bit like an onion, as shown schematically in Figure F-1, where "...." represents layers of elements between oxygen and iron. This image is idealized; in reality, the layers are not all equally thick, and turbulence prevents different elements from separating completely.

Each fusion cycle releases less energy than its predecessors, and ends much sooner.

For a star with 25 times the mass of our Sun, four key fusion cycles, their core temperatures, and the cycle durations are:

Cycle	Core Temp.	Duration
Hydrogen to Helium	100 M K	7 M yrs
Helium to Carbon	400 M K	500,000 yrs
Carbon to Oxygen	1,700 M K	600 yrs
Silicon to Iron	7,000 M K	1 day

In this table, M denotes million, and K denotes degrees above absolute zero (the Kelvin scale). These temperatures in °F are roughly twice the Kelvin values.

Less massive stars burn much slower, and live much longer.

Our Sun burns 36,000 times less fuel each second than does a star that is 25 times more massive. As a result, our Sun will remain in its hydrogen fusion cycle for 10 billion years, much longer than the 7 million years shown in the table above. We are now roughly midway through our Sun's hydrogen fusion cycle.

Our Sun is the ideal type of star. It provides a long and stable environment in which life can develop.

Further Reading

For more about Dr. Piccioni, his books, podcast radio shows, and newsletters, visit his website:

www.guidetothecosmos.com

For more about the fine-tuning of our universe, visit:

www.guidetothecosmos/acclife.html

For more about *Our Place in The Universe*, visit:
www.guidetothecosmos.com/series02.html

For more about the Cosmic Microwave Background, visit:

www.guidetothecosmos.com/Singles/CMB-WMAP.
html

For more about the age of the Earth, visit:
www.guidetothecosmos.com/series07.html

eBooks by Robert L. Piccioni

- Feynman Simplified: 1A through 3C
- Math for Physicists (Feynman Simplified: 4A)
- Feynman's Best (Feynman Simplified: 4B)
- Special Relativity: 1, 2, 3
- General Relativity: 1, 2, 3, 4, 5
- A World Without Einstein
- Einstein: Rejection, Persistence, Success
- Quantum Mechanics: 1, 2, 3, 4, 5
- Our Place in the Universe
- Our Universe: 1, 2, 3, 4, 5
- Higgs & Bosons & Fermions...Oh My!
- Black Holes, Supernovae & More
- Science & Faith
- Timeless Atoms
- We are Stardust
- Searching for Earth 2.0
- Smarter Energy

Print Books by Robert L. Piccioni

- Everyone's Guide to Atoms, Einstein,
  and the Universe
- Einstein's Theories of Relativity
- Feynman Simplified Parts 1, 2, 3
- Math for Physicists and Feynman's Best
  combined as Feynman Simplified Part 4
- Can Life Be Merely An Accident?
- Science & Faith
- A World Without Einstein

Dr. Robert L. Piccioni is a physicist, author, educator, radio show host, and high-tech entrepreneur. He explains the wonders of science at high schools, universities, churches, business groups, civic organizations, astronomy clubs, adult education programs, and cruise ships. He has a B.S. degree from  Caltech, where one of his professors was Nobel Laureate Richard Feynman, and a Ph.D. degree in high-energy physics from Stanford University, where his thesis advisor was Nobel Laureate Melvin Schwartz. He was on the research faculty of Harvard University working with Nobel Laureate Carlo Rubbia.

Robert was a principal of eight high-tech companies and holds patents in medical, microelectronics, and smart energy technologies.

Now "retired", Dr. Piccioni teaches at the Osher Institute at UCLA and CSUCI, where students voted him "Teacher of the Year."

Robert presents *Real Science for Real People*, making the key facts and concepts of science understandable without "dumbing" them down. He is the author of 9 print books and 41 ebooks; half are intended for the general public, and half for physics students.

Robert likes to say: You don't have to be a great musician to appreciate great music. Nor do you need to be a great scientist to appreciate the exciting discoveries and intriguing mysteries of our universe.

Made in the USA
Middletown, DE
08 January 2023

20914571R00061